# 30 Days

## To Overcome

# Regret

*A Mindfulness Program with a Touch of Humor*

Harper Daniels

Copyright © JV 2021

## Share your journey!

Let people know you're practicing mindfulness! Post a picture of the cover and include #30DaysNow via social media. Our various guides share the same lessons, so you can see how others are using mindfulness on their journey!

Don't forget that each exercise has a unique hashtag for online sharing.

This book is meant to be a guide only, and does not guarantee specific results. If the lessons and exercises in this book are followed, change can occur for certain people. Results vary from person to person; some people may not need to complete the thirty days to experience change, but it's encouraged that the entire program be read completely through at least once.

The last half of the book consists of blank note pages that the reader can use in conjunction with the exercises for each day. The reader is encouraged to utilize the note pages; though it's not necessary.

**Give the gift of mindfulness.** See similar guides at www.30DaysNow.com if you wish to purchase a book for a loved one. **See the disclosure below.**

### Disclosure (Shared Lessons and Exercises):
Keep in mind that our mindfulness guides share the same lessons and exercises, so there is no need to purchase more than one book; unless you are sharing with a group or giving the guides as gifts. Our mindfulness guides are created for various topics; however, they utilize the same lessons and exercises, so please be aware of this before purchasing. For example, *30 Days to Overcome Regret* will mostly have the same lessons and exercises as *30 Days to Overcome Guilt* and so forth. By reading just one of our guides, you'll be able to apply the same lessons and exercises to multiple areas of your life.

Enjoy your journey of self-discovery!

# Contents

Preface..................................................4

Day 1....................................................7
Day 2....................................................8
Day 3....................................................9
Day 4...................................................10
Day 5...................................................11
Day 6...................................................12
Day 7...................................................13
Day 8...................................................14
Day 9...................................................15
Day 10..................................................16
Day 11..................................................17
Day 12..................................................18
Day 13..................................................19
Day 14..................................................20
Day 15..................................................21
Day 16..................................................22
Day 17..................................................23
Day 18..................................................24
Day 19..................................................25
Day 20..................................................26
Day 21..................................................27
Day 22..................................................28
Day 23..................................................29
Day 24..................................................30
Day 25..................................................31
Day 26..................................................32
Day 27..................................................33
Day 28..................................................34
Day 29..................................................35
Day 30..................................................36

Conclusion.............................................37
Note Pages...........................Begins on 39

# Preface

Did you know that more people regret what they didn't do, than what they had done? Regret is a remarkable condition. It's an anguish that is wrapped in shame, bitterness, and sometimes grief. Though it appears to have a lot of power, regret can be easily overcome, as this 30 days mindfulness program will reveal to you. Life is not meant to be spent believing the lies of regret. If you struggle with regret, it's time to drop the attachment.

Regret is essentially a misperception of experiences and time; in other words, regret sends the message that you could have, should have, or shouldn't have done something in the past. With regret, the blame is placed entirely on you; as if you're in control of the universal past and present. Let's not forget, the past is always an illusion – the only time that ever was is now, at this moment. We'll get more into that philosophy later.

For the purpose of this book let's define *regret* as: an adverse attachment to the belief that your present moment experience could be better if you had made different choices or decisions in the past. You can use this definition of regret; however, feel free to define *regret* any way you wish based on your unique individualistic experience. However you define it, just realize that regret is an attachment to a misconception of control and time.

People experience regret for various reasons: not traveling to a particular place, not pursuing a certain opportunity, staying in a boring job, not having children, not committing to a certain relationship, not studying a topic of interest, committing an act of hate or aggression, treating another person with disdain, maintaining a bad habit…the list is endless. For whatever reason you're participating in this mindfulness program, it is very possible to drop the attachment to regret and move on in the present moment, fully aware and happy.

The following pages involve a 30 day mindfulness program made up of lessons and exercises to help you overcome patterns of thinking, feelings, and attachments that have kept you stuck in regret. Though these lessons and exercises can be applied to any unhealthy reliance, this program will focus specifically on the experience of regret.

For some readers, they'll overcome the old reliance quickly and will drop the pernicious thoughts and dependency in no time; and for others, they'll overcome regret slowly and gradually. In either case, if you stick with the program, you'll start to witness the effects of regret weaken. Please don't judge your progress in the program, as this isn't a competition and there isn't a goal you must attain. Let the debilitating thoughts, feelings, habits, and attachment simply drop as you work through the exercises and lessons.

It's not necessary to complete the program's days in order, nor should you be religious about completing them successfully. There is no such thing as a successful completion of this program. The bottom line is to observe and awaken, and that cannot be obtained through success, force, pressure, struggle, or competition. Simply relax, follow the program, and the attachment will loosen.

You'll also notice that mindfulness, silence, and stillness are a regular discipline for each day in the program. Because you've been influenced by a dependency based society that demands instant gratification, silence and stillness may seem nearly impossible for you to practice. For this reason, we'll incorporate this discipline from the outset. A quiet and still mind is an incredibly powerful resource, but one that requires daily maintenance.

It should also be noted that you're not required to fight the feelings of regret during the program; however, if you've already dropped the attachment, then do not pick it up again. The point being: by practicing the following exercises and lessons in the days to come, you won't even need willpower to move on from regret – it'll just happen.

You'll need about 15-30 minutes per day for the program; but feel free to spend more time if needed. The amount of time doesn't matter, as long as you're in an environment that allows you to concentrate without distraction. Also to be mentioned, the last portion of this book includes note pages that you can use with the exercises. It's encouraged that you write down any thoughts, insights, adaptations, lessons, mantras, etc, on those blank pages. The note pages can also be used to rip out and take with you. Feel free to use them as you wish.

One last thing: If you're like most people, you might be dependent on caffeine, alcohol, or sugar to some extent. If you are, do your best to lessen the consumption of these substances over the next 30 days. It's not necessary that you abstain, but can you cut consumption of these substances in half, or more? It's important that your mind is sober and your body relaxed to make the most of these exercises and lessons.

Let's get started.

*Let others know you're practicing mindfulness! Post a picture of the cover and include #30DaysNow. Also, don't forget that each exercise has a unique hashtag for online sharing.*

# Day 1

(Share this experience using #30DaysBreathing)

Exercise:

*Find a place without distraction, and turn off all electronics. Sit with your back straight, kneel, or lie on a hard surface (not bed) and remain in silence for 10 minutes.*

*During these 10 minutes, take deep and focused breaths and hold them for a few seconds each. Exhale slowly. Listen intently to your breathing. Don't try to change it – simply listen, and feel the air go in and out.*

*When you're ready, repeat the mantra: "**Be still. Be silent.**" Repeat this slowly multiple times out loud as well as quietly. You might experience boredom or anxiety, but continue repeating the mantra regardless. Repeat it until you're calm and focused. You can continue the deep breathing during the mantra, or take deep breaths during pauses. Don't rush.*

Each of the 30 days will have this time of silence, focused breathing, and a mantra. Except for this page, the end of each day will remind you of the minutes you are to spend in silence and focused breathing; and will also have a mantra for you to practice. You can repeat the mantras during your times of silence and focused breathing, or following. Remember, there is no right or wrong way to do this.

Adverse thoughts and feelings want to fight; in fact, they're energized by fighting. Instead of fighting regret, meet it with silence and observation. Let the exercises and lessons in this program guide you.

# Day 2

(Share this experience using #30DaysPonder)

Exercise:

*Ponder this question: Can you remember a point in your life when you lived happily without regret?*

Writing is extremely beneficial to the mind; especially when pondering. Write down your thoughts about this particular question. If your mind drifts, then write whatever thoughts emerge. It's okay if you have nothing to write, but ponder the question regardless.

Were you able to remember a period in your life when you weren't experiencing regret? If you're like many people, you may have to return to memories of childhood to determine that period. It's not uncommon for a person to experience regret early on, and continue experiencing it throughout life. We're taught early, in school and family, to be regretful for perceived misdeeds; and as a result, the attachment to regret is born. Remember, regret is a lie based on a misperception of time and control – both of which are illusions. Most everyone is taught to feel regret for something happening or not happening; however, it's not necessary to keep the attachment.

Recognize that regret is a learned misperception with roots. However, it can be dropped quickly and completely; and you have the capability to drop it. In other words, you are not controlled, identified, or dominated by a learned misconception of past and present conditions.

*10 minutes of silence and focused breathing. Repeat the mantra: **"Drop. Unlearn. Discover."**

# Day 3

(Share this experience using #30DaysLies)

Exercise:

*On a sheet of paper (any size) write down all the internal lies that you regularly hear about yourself – i.e. within your mind.*

*Now, tear the paper into multiple pieces, and throw away.*

It's common to have an internal voice (or voices) within your mind, playing a record of lies over and over. We eventually begin to accept these lies and let them impact our growth and happiness. Most people you see on a daily basis have these recurring internal voices; and most people are oblivious to them – sort of like white noise. This isn't a mental illness, but a way in which the mind works. We all experience these internal quiet voices whispering untruths about our being. These lies are nothing to fear, but they need to be observed. Writing them down can help you observe and become aware of their deceptions.

The power of silence, focused breathing, and mantras, which you have been practicing, is to draw out the lies. Let them manifest, and observe them. Common internal lies include: *"You're guilty," "You're a failure," "You're a bad person," "You don't measure up," "They'll never forgive you," "You don't deserve to be free,"* and so on. These thoughts are not part of you; however, the deception is to make you believe they are. Regret can implant many of these lies clandestinely.

*10 minutes of silence and focused breathing. Repeat the mantra: **"Thoughts are only thoughts - nothing more."**

# Day 4

(Share this experience using #30DaysHandcuffs)

Exercise:

*Put your wrists together. Press them tight together as if they're locked by handcuffs. Actually imagine handcuffs around your wrists.*

*Now, separate your wrists as if the handcuffs were released or broken – you can do this quickly or slowly.*

Guilt implies that you were judged by an authority and were found to be at fault for a crime or misdeed. However, even those who are placed in actual handcuffs are innocent until proven guilty in a court of law. So why do most people accept guilt from others, who are not in a position of authority? Understand; no one makes you feel guilty – it's entirely you shackling yourself. Anyone who attempts to make you feel guilty has guilt of their own to deal with; don't accept it. Regret feeds of this illusive guilt.

Feeling guilty is the same as placing yourself in imaginary handcuffs and assigning yourself to an emotional prison cell. Don't do that any longer. Many people are taught to assign and accept guilt based on absolutely nothing; most of this deception is learned from childhood, when parents and those in assumed authority threaten punishment and scold. Don't confuse guilt with shame. Unless you committed an actual crime, there is no reason to accept guilt. Drop the illusion. Break free from your illusory handcuffs, and live without regret.

*10 minutes of silence and focused breathing. Repeat the mantra: **"I am not bound by guilt or regret. I am free."**

# Day 5
(Share this experience using #30DaysTrash)

Exercise:

*Go out and buy a small trash can. You should be able to find one cheaply. If you don't have the funds for this exercise, you can use an empty box or container; however, a small trash can works better for its symbolism.*

*Designate this specific trash can your "concerns and worries can" (or use any title you wish) – some people benefit from writing this label directly onto the can.*

*Now, write down (on scraps of paper or whatever paper you wish to use) any concerns, worries, and adverse thoughts that you may be experiencing today, and throw them into the can. Try to practice this every day: quickly write down worries, concerns, and negative thoughts, and then throw them into the can. It may be beneficial to have a supply of scrap paper near the can for easy access.*

This exercise may seem simple, but let's go beyond throwing your written concerns, worries, and thoughts away. Designate a few times during the week for sifting through the can and taking out random worries and concerns from days prior – just reach in and pull some out. Observe them, but don't judge yourself. This is a great exercise to learn your negative thought patterns and the lies that grip your conscience. If you stick with this practice, you may gain a deeper understanding and realization into the dependencies, habits, thought patterns, and feelings that have you experiencing regret.

*10 minutes of silence and focused breathing. Repeat the mantra: **"There is nothing to worry about. All is well."**

# Day 6

(Share this experience using #30DaysGrip)

Exercise:

*Find a hard object that you can hold in the palm of your hand (such as a stone, ball, or bottle). With either hand, grip this object tightly and squeeze it as hard as you can. Squeeze it forcefully until you can't hold on to it any longer. Drop the object when ready.*

If you could continue squeezing that object forever, perhaps you would; but your muscles and nerves can only endure for so long. At some point, you simply and quickly release the grip and drop the object. There isn't a process to the drop; it just happens when your body says that's enough. The release happens naturally without effort.

Letting go of an unhealthy dependency, habit, thought pattern, addiction, emotion, or behavior can be that easy. Letting go can be as natural and regret-free as dropping the object you were gripping onto so tightly in this exercise; so, take a lesson from your body's experience. When it's time to let go, then let go. The time to let go of regret is always now. Just let the drop happen.

Regret can have a whimsical hold on your life – it's an illusion and false perception. Let it go; and live your life in the present moment, free and happy. Surround yourself with reminders to experience the present moment.

*10 minutes of silence and focused breathing. Repeat the mantra: **"Letting go is natural. I can let go, here and now."**

# Day 7

(Share this experience using #30DaysPassing)

Exercise:

*On a piece of paper (any size) write down the name of your current emotion. For example, at this moment you might be feeling agitated, calm, bored, angry, anxious, excited, etc. Whatever emotion you are experiencing, give it a name and put it on paper.*

*Now, write down "I'm experiencing this emotion in the present moment and it will pass. It's only an emotion."*

*You can throw the paper away, or hold onto it if you wish.*

Similar to how we give certain words credence, we tend to give our emotions a lot of trust. We also tend to blame the outside world for emotions we are feeling: *"They made me angry," "I'm depressed because they made me feel guilty,"* or, *"If they gave me the job, I would be happy."*

The emotions you feel are in you, not in the outer world. No one can cause you to feel or emote in a particular way; if they're able to, it's only because you let them. A great way to let a harmful emotion pass is to observe it; and a good start is by giving it a name and seeing it as powerless.

It's commonplace to blame others for our pain. Instead of seeing the emotion for what it is and letting it pass, we've been taught to rely on attachments, like regret, to manage the emotional reaction. Wake up! Emotions are not you.

*10 minutes of silence and focused breathing. Repeat the mantra: **"I am not an emotion. All emotions that I experience will pass."**

# Day 8

(Share this experience using #30DaysDoorway)

Exercise:

*Stand in front of a doorway, with the door open. Close your eyes, and take a deep breath. With eyes closed and holding your breath, step through the doorway. Once you have stepped through completely, open your eyes and exhale.*

Doorways offer great lessons for practicing mindfulness and observation. How often do you rush through doors without paying attention to the change of environment? We don't often pay attention or appreciate the transition; we simply rush through unaware that our perspective has changed. This isn't a bad thing; in fact, it's great that we don't stall in front of doorways, too afraid to enter the next environment. At the beginning of this exercise you were in a particular place, and then you stepped through a doorway into a completely different setting. You made a transition without worry or concern, and very naturally. The transition to a permanent regret-free experience is that easy.

When it comes to physical doorways, we rarely stop and worry about the change of environment – we just walk through and accept the new experience. You can apply this same lesson to decisions that have you stressed, anxious, or worried regarding regret. Step through the decision to be regret-free and accept the changes; but try to step through aware and grateful. There will always be a doorway leading to new experiences. When you drop the illusion of regret, doorways will be present.

*10 minutes of silence and focused breathing. Repeat the mantra: **"I accept change with awareness and gratitude."**

# Day 9

(Share this experience using #30DaysIdentity)

Exercise:

*On a piece of paper, write down all the labels and adjectives that you and others use to identify you.*

For example, do you see yourself as a daughter, son, mother, father, student, teacher, cashier, friend, engineer, accountant, employee, employer, roommate, wife, husband, etc? And what adjectives do you use to label yourself; for example, do you identify yourself as failed, successful, happy, depressed, moral, unethical, lustful, greedy, valuable, worthless, etc? Don't only write down the labels and descriptions you perceive; but also write down what you believe others label you as: do you believe others see you as a complainer, strong motivator, valuable friend, stupid and incompetent employee, extremely smart and talented worker, etc? Take as long as you need, and fill up a sheet of paper with those labels and descriptions.

After you've done that, tear the paper into multiple pieces and throw it away. Those labels and adjectives mean nothing. They're not *you*. You cannot be defined, labeled, described, or controlled by titles. Most people poison their conscience with such learned vocabulary. They really believe these words hold power – they'll even fight, stress out, become ill, and die to make these words part of reality. Regret, as well as most unhealthy misconceptions, teaches you to identify with particular words, which are only thoughts. Unlearn them.

*10 minutes of silence and focused breathing. Repeat the mantra: **"*I am not a label, title, or description.*"**

# Day 10
(Share this experience using #30DaysFocus)

Exercise:

*Focus on a natural object or scene for 10 minutes, without distraction and in silence.*

Focusing on a natural object for an extended period of time is an ancient practice. How often have you stopped to observe something objectively for more than 10 minutes? When was the last time you've quietly watched a sunset, sunrise, tree sway in the wind, bird chirping, clouds passing or expanding, or just a rock? That might sound boring, but this practice is very liberating. If you look at anything long enough, you start to see it from a different perspective. As easy as this exercise sounds, it's not – try it out, and see how long you can observe without thoughts impeding the practice.

Watching a bird feed may be more interesting than watching an immobile rock; but I encourage you to start with an immobile object, such as a stone or piece of wood. During this process thoughts will emerge – observe the thoughts and let them pass. Don't attach a goal or benchmark of success to this exercise; just observe an object.

The ultimate goal of regret is to hypnotize you with a false narrative; stealing your attention from the present moment. Wake up to what's around you in the present. Don't let regret steal present moment awareness from you.

*10 minutes of silence and focused breathing. Repeat the mantra: **"Be focused. Observe. Be present."**

# Day 11
(Share this experience using #30DaysWalk)

Exercise:

*Go for a mindfulness walk for at least 10 minutes. Focus on each step. Feel the steps: the feel of your feet hitting the ground, your heel rolling forward, your toes, the bend of your knees, your hips working to balance your posture, the swinging of your arms, etc. Don't rush; go slow. Focus on your breathing as well. Get in tune with your body. Pay attention to your physical senses throughout the walk. Focus – don't listen to music or be distracted.*

Human beings have always used walking as a naturally restorative exercise. There is something about walking, and focusing on the walk, that calms the mind and soul. The longer one walks, the more relaxed one feels.

Any moment is a good time to walk and experience your inner and outer environment. During long walks, thoughts will emerge that will allow you to consciously observe them. Let the thoughts pass; you may even have emotions that emerge, observe those and let them pass as well. Focusing on your steps will help you clear the mind of clutter. Walking in the early morning and at dusk is especially beneficial.

A 20 minute walk brings more comfort, stillness, peace, focus, and awareness than hundreds of hours ruminating with regret. Walk every day, as much as you can. Walk the deceit of regret away.

*10 minutes of silence and focused breathing. Repeat the mantra: *"I am relaxed. I am at peace."*

# Day 12
(Share this experience using #30DaysBreak)

Exercise:

*Find an object that you can break: an egg, a drinking glass, a pencil...anything. In a safe place, break the object of your choice, and be especially careful if it's glass or something sharp.*

*Don't clean up the pieces immediately, observe the mess and let the pieces sit for at least a few minutes.*

Did you break the object, or did I break the object by directing you to break it? And if you believe it was only you who broke the object, did the object allow you to break it? This isn't an exercise meant to release frustration or stress. The purpose of this lesson is to show you that you're not 100% responsible for your perceived chaos, mess, loss, failure, or broken pieces.

Destruction happens in the present moment, and that's OK. We spend so much time worrying about the future, goals, relationships, plans, jobs, situations, and other things breaking into pieces. And when that happens, we tend to blame ourselves or others, because that's what we've been taught to do. Allow breaking to happen; and observe the pieces as well as your reaction to the destruction. Regret can feel like shattered pieces of image, reputation, self, ego, and character...so what? Let the breaking occur. Observe the pieces, and smile at them. Broken pieces don't validate regret.

*10 minutes of silence and focused breathing. Repeat the mantra: **"I cannot harm or break the present moment."**

# Day 13
(Share this experience using #30DaysSmile)

Exercise:

*Hold a smile for 5 minutes. You don't need to do this exercise in front of a mirror; but feel free to do so if you wish. You can even do this exercise during the 10 minutes of silence and focused breathing. While holding your smile, take a moment and feel your face; actually touch the smile and the curvature of your lips and cheek bones.*

Have you ever behaved a certain way and then saw your mood change immediately? Physical exercise, such as running and weightlifting, does this for many people. Certain forms of yoga have also been used by people to change their moods. The point is: changing your behavior not only impacts other people, but can also impact your perception of yourself.

You'll notice that while you're smiling during this exercise, you may experience certain emotions. You might feel silly, embarrassed, stupid, weird, or whatever. Continue smiling regardless. In fact, if you're still experiencing adverse feelings from regret at this point, smile while you're in the grips of them – hold the smile as long as you can; set a reminder alarm if needed. As always, observe your thoughts while you're smiling; observe the thoughts as if they're clouds passing by in a bright blue sky.

Smiling causes an authentic reaction in our bodies and minds that is essentially good. The present moment enjoys a nice smile. So practice holding that smile, even when feeling regretful.

*10 minutes of silence and focused breathing. Repeat the mantra: *"Happiness is now. I am happy."*

# Day 14

(Share this experience using #30DaysMyLabel)

Exercise:

*Most food products have a "Nutritious Facts" label that will tell you the percentage of fat, cholesterol, sodium, carbohydrates, protein, and other important nutritious content in the product. Let's make one for your experience.*

*On a sheet of paper, write down the words: happiness, stress, anxiety, worry, anger, and depression. Feel free to add other words that describe emotions and feelings that you may regularly experience. Now, next to each word write down the percentages that best represent their measure in your life. There is no right or wrong for this exercise; the point is to become keenly aware of what emotions and feelings you are experiencing more often than others. If you write 70% depression, that is not "bad". Simply be honest with the percentages; recognize them.*

Which emotions received the highest percentages? Which received the lowest? Remember, you are not your emotions or feelings; however, you do experience emotions and feelings, and some of them will be experienced more than others, especially during misperceived regret. If you are experiencing adverse emotions more often than positive ones, then don't let that bother you. Whatever emotion you experience in the present moment, observe it and let it pass. For the negative emotions that come regularly, examine them and let them fade. Observation is the key to understanding.

*10 minutes of silence and focused breathing. Repeat the mantra: **"I am not ruled by emotion. I am here and now."**

# Day 15

(Share this experience using #30DaysEnd)

Exercise:

*Choose a book; perhaps one that you have at home that you haven't read in a while, or from the library. You can also use a long article for this exercise. It's best if you haven't read the book or article beforehand.*

*Now, instead of reading from the beginning; read the last chapter (or paragraph if it's an article) first.*

Does this go against your conventional way of perceiving a story? Did you feel that it's pointless to even read the entire book, or article, since you're aware of its ending before reading the beginning? Just because you started at the end of the book doesn't impact the story; instead, it impacts your perception.

If you've been struggling with a particular problem, situation, or difficulty in life; is it the beginning, middle, or end of your dilemma? This isn't to teach you that you can control the end or beginning of an experience; because you can't. The purpose is to show you that the present moment is all you'll ever need, and you can accept the end as the beginning and the beginning as the end, if that's your experience in the present moment. So, be open to perceive all things as they are now, with or without a beginning or end. In other words, be awake, don't worry, and be happy…without regret.

*15 minutes of silence and focused breathing. Repeat the mantra: **"There is no end or beginning. There's only ever now."**

# Day 16
(Share this experience using #30DaysCoffin)

Exercise:

*Lay down on the floor (not on a bed or couch), with your back straight and your arms at your side. Close your eyes.*

*Now, imagine yourself in a coffin or under the ground. If this depresses you, do it regardless. With your eyes closed, imagine not being able to open them ever again; also imagine not being able to move your body or speaking ever again. Stay in this position for 10 minutes, or as long as you can.*

If this seems gothic or dark, that's only your learned perception of the death experience. There's an ancient teaching that says the way to enlightenment is through a keen awareness of death. The person who is daily reminded that the body will die, and faces this fact head on with a clear mind and acceptance, has nothing to lose and is truly free to live in the present moment. The question isn't whether or not your body will die (because it surely will); the more important question is will you live before death?

Will you truly live before your body dies? The present moment is the only thing you'll always experience. Instead of fearing a pending death, accept it and be thankful for the present moment; and live in it, free of regret!

*15 minutes of silence and focused breathing. Repeat the mantra: **"My body will age and pass, but I will always be present - free from regret."**

# Day 17

(Share this experience using #30DaysLose)

Exercise:

*Choose an object that you use and rely on every day, and that you sometimes lose – such as a key, cell phone, pen, hat, toothbrush, or television controller.*

*Now, actually attempt to lose this object. Hide it well, and try to make yourself forget where it is.*

More than likely you won't be able to lose this object, as hard as you try, because you have applied a lot of attention to the process of losing it and trying to make yourself forget. At this point, losing it is nearly impossible. Why do you think this is?

If you try to drop a dependency, behavior, thought pattern, addiction, or any unhealthy vice using a lot of thought, attention, focus, struggle, and effort…you'll never lose it. It will be with you in one form or another for a very long time, possibly forever. The point is: whatever you give attention to consistently, will be difficult to lose. This is the reason why people who complain a lot are never happy – they can't stop giving thought and attention to the problems they're grumbling about. The problems eventually become an intimate part of their lives. Remember, rival enemies maintain a devoted relationship.

Don't think about the things you regret; don't fight or oppose the thoughts. Let the misperception be forgotten, and thus lost.

*15 minutes of silence and focused breathing. Repeat the mantra: **"I do not need to hold on. I allow it to be lost."**

# Day 18
### (Share this experience using #30DaysGSR)

Exercise:

*Say the words "Guilt", "Shame", and "Regret" 10 times to yourself out loud. Don't rush. Pause between each repetition. For the pause, you can take a deep breath. Your eyes can remain open or closed. Again, don't rush - say the words slowly and observe any thoughts, feelings, or images that emerge internally.*

*Now, say these words again 10 times, but with a smile.*

What futile credence we give words such as Guilt, Shame and Regret. We use these words on ourselves as well as others; they become regular vocabulary for our internal recurring voices. And in the end, they're mere words that hold no power. What would these words be without a facial expression, tone, inflection, or emphasis?

When you said these three specific words, what thoughts came to mind, what did you feel, and was there a reaction in your body? If there is a reaction, such as shortness of breath or a frown, people tend to interpret it as sadness; but this reaction is a learned behavior. We've been taught to feel and think a certain way with regard to guilt, shame, and regret. The truth is: these words mean nothing.

Regret, like most adverse ideas, flourishes on these three words and the learned reactions they produce. But see them for what they are…mere words with no power.

*15 minutes of silence and focused breathing. Repeat the mantra: **"I am not Guilt, Shame, or Regret."**

# Day 19

(Share this experience using #30DaysBadSupport)

Exercise:

*On a sheet of paper, large enough to make a list, write down the self-defeating thoughts that you regularly experience - these are the thoughts that act as internal voices telling you who are, who you are not, and what you should or should not be doing. Such thoughts may include, "You're not worth it", "You're a loser," "You'll never change", "You should be doing better," "You should have done...," or "You shouldn't have done..."*

*Now, next to these pernicious thoughts, write the names of the people in your life who you believe would agree with or support them in one way or another.*

We all experience internal voices that are not beneficial to our present moment experience. Most of these internal voices have been with us for a while – it is completely normal to have them. However, you must recognize that these negative recurrent thoughts are not *you*. They can be dropped when observed and identified.

Often times, the people in our lives either support or oppose our negative internal voices. Identify which individuals in your life support, directly or indirectly, these lies; and identify those individuals who oppose them. The company you keep is critical. Ensure that your close relationships are positive. Don't allow any support of recurrent self-harming internal voices.

*15 minutes of silence and focused breathing. Repeat the mantra: **"I am not an internal negative voice. Such thoughts have no control over my happiness."**

# Day 20
(Share this experience using #30DaysSymbol)

Exercise:

*Choose a physical symbol that will remind you to observe and be aware in the present moment. Try to choose something from nature, or that is made of natural material.*

The object you choose can be anything, but it's best if it's something that you can enjoy looking at and touching. For example, many walkers and hikers will find a unique rock small enough to carry in their hands. A stone, necklace, bracelet, seashell, cedar block, coin…anything will do, as long as you enjoy it and you can dedicate it as a tool for remembrance.

Another cunning trick of regret is to confuse the mind into forgetting you're part of the natural world. The illusion of regret preys on, manipulates, and influences the imagination. Thus, you're taken out of physical reality. By having a symbol of remembrance, you can reconnect with the present moment. This symbol isn't meant to be an idol, god, or icon. Don't think too deeply into this. The symbol is simply a tool to help you remember where you are in the here and now. As long as you're aware of the present, you'll have no desire to return to the hallucination that accompanies regret.

*15 minutes of silence and focused breathing. Repeat the mantra: **"All is well. Here and now, all is well."**

# Day 21
(Share this experience using #30DaysCoin)

Exercise:

*Find a coin. While standing, flip the coin and let it land wherever. If it lands with the head side up, spin around to the right until you come back to your original place; if it lands tail side up, spin around to the left until you come back to your original place. Again, head side up, spin to the right; tail side up, spin to the left – doing a full circle until you return to your original standing position.*

In which direction did you spin? In this exercise you left the direction of your movement completely up to the flip, the coin, and gravity. When you spun, you experienced a specific visual perception of the environment that you would not have had from spinning in the opposite direction. But, you returned to the original position regardless, full circle.

The experience would have been different if you spun to the opposite side; and if you repeat this exercise multiple times, your experiences in the same direction will be different as well. The point being: it doesn't matter what direction you go in or what you experience; you'll always return to the present moment; so the time to be awake, aware, and regret-free is always now.

The message of regret is, *"You should have (or shouldn't have) gone in that direction!"* This is a complete lie. There only ever was the present moment; so enjoy it right now.

*15 minutes of silence and focused breathing. Repeat the mantra: *"The direction does not matter. I am always here and now, in the present moment."*

# Day 22

(Share this experience using #30DaysHobby)

Exercise:

*On a sheet of paper (one that you can easily save and return to later) make a list of hobbies that you've had in the past but have neglected, and also make a list of hobbies that you would like to start in the future.*

*From these lists choose one hobby from the past and one new hobby that you'd like to start. Focus only on these two – the old hobby and the new one. Make this a priority.*

How often have you said, or have heard other people say, "*I wish I had the time.*" You do have the time. You just choose to think of time in the way that you've been taught to perceive it. If your life depended on it, you would certainly make the time if needed.

In fact, time is a manmade construct - don't ever forget that. There is only the present moment. Past and future are not here and now. We spend far too much time thinking about time. How many of your recurrent inner thoughts involve questions such as, "*When will that ever happen?*" "*When will I ever change?*" "*Why did that have to happen?*" "*If the past were different, life would be better.*" These are lies that only eat into the present moment, and infect our modern world.

Regret occupies the present moment; and that moment can be used to pursue hobbies that magnify your happiness.

*15 minutes of silence and focused breathing. Repeat the mantra: "***The time is now. Happiness is present.***"

# Day 23

(Share this experience using #30DaysPinch)

Exercise:

*Pinch the skin on the back of your hand or forearm until there is discomfort and slight pain. It's not necessary to pinch hard enough to bruise yourself, just enough to feel a small burn.*

Did I cause the pain by asking you to do this exercise? No; you caused this pain to yourself – think about this carefully. You even decided how much pain to give yourself, and when to relieve the pain. You can't blame me or anyone else for the pain you just experienced. You were solely responsible. You were also responsible for letting go.

This is easily understood with regard to physical pain, such as pinching oneself; however, we have a lot of difficulty understanding this lesson as it applies to adverse emotions and feelings. How often have you said, and have heard others say, *"He makes me so angry when..."*, *"I'm depressed because she..."*, or *"I'm so frustrated that they..."* No person ever makes you experience negative feelings. It's always you who are experiencing them; and then placing the blame on others. Essentially, you are emotionally pinching yourself and not letting go. People go their entire lives without releasing the pinch. Instead of letting go, they scream at others, *"Release the pain! Let go! Fix this! Stop this! You're to blame!"* Wake up and see that you are solely responsible for letting go of the pain, and you can do it now. No one is to blame for misperceived regret, and the feelings that accompany it. Release the pinch.

*15 minutes of silence and focused breathing. Repeat the mantra: *"I can release negative feelings, here and now."*

# Day 24
(Share this experience using #30DaysGoals)

Exercise:

*On a piece of paper (any size) write down the goals that you've been striving to achieve – i.e. the goals that you believe will bring you fulfillment. For example: a new job, a house in a nice neighborhood, traveling the world, a business, a family, new friends, a degree or certification, building a network, reaching a net worth of a million dollars, etc.*

*Now, tear up the paper into multiple pieces and throw away.*

Goals can be very helpful and useful if they're not obsessed over. However, in the modern world people develop a reliance on goals. Think about all the times you've said something like, *"I need to get that," "I must reach this," "I'll do anything to accomplish that"*, etc. It's often the case that people spend more time worrying about their goals, than freely doing something in the present moment to reach them. Plus, the goal in itself is fleeting, while the journey in the present moment is real and lasting.

The habit of thinking that goals must be met, or else failure ensues, is subtly fixed to dependencies. When you experience regret, what goals accompany the lie? What was it that you felt you needed to achieve?

*15 minutes of silence and focused breathing. Repeat the mantra: *"**My happiness does not depend on meeting a goal. I'm happy now.**"

# Day 25
### (Share this experience using #30DaysDance)
Exercise:

*With or without music, spend 5-10 minutes dancing. If you are too shy or embarrassed to dance, remember that you'll be alone – so there won't be anyone judging your amazing, or lack of amazing, dance skills. You can even do this exercise from a seated position or during your time of meditation by moving your arms and hands to any rhythm you like. Music is not necessary.*

Dancing is universally accepted as a language of happiness. Not only is dancing healthy for the body, but it is very beneficial to the mind. Something happens to the mind when you dance that is mystical and healing. Dancing with another person or group is wonderful, but dancing solo is extraordinary. The person who dances alone, aware of the body's sensations and movements and totally content in the present moment, can experience an enlightened state of being.

Life is similar to a dance. It flows, speeds up, slows down, changes direction, goes off beat, has a beginning, and has an end. When you're dancing, reflect on your life as a dance – don't judge it, just observe your life as a beautiful dance, regardless of its course and rhythm.

*15 minutes of silence and focused breathing. Repeat the mantra: **"Life is a dance, and I am always in rhythm."**

# Day 26
### (Share this experience using #30DaysWorstCase)
Exercise:

*Think of a major worry that consistently upsets you. On a sheet of paper, write down three worst case scenarios for that dominating concern. For example, if someone is persistently worried about failing a specific job, that individual can write as a worst case scenario, "I will do poorly at the job, and will be fired; leaving me homeless and broke." As mentioned, write down three worst case scenarios for your particular worry.*

*Now, next to each of those three worst case scenarios write, "I accept this." You can either toss the paper or keep it.*

Worry is an illness that goes untreated in most people, especially when experiencing regret. Think of worry like a cancer of the spirit; but few people know how to treat it effectively. One of the only ways to eradicate worry isn't to fight, ignore, or run from it; but to face it in the present moment and accept it for the illusion it is. You can never be worried about something happening in the present moment – that's impossible; you can only be worried about the future, which is always illusory.

Writing down your worries and worst case scenarios, if they ever do come true (which they rarely do), is a great way to draw those thoughts out of your mind and into the present moment, allowing you to face, accept, and observe them. Accept the worst case scenarios that regret throws at you; knowing that the odds of them happening are slim.

*15 minutes of silence and focused breathing. Repeat the mantra: **"Worries are not real. They are only thoughts."**

# Day 27
(Share this experience using #30DaysStack)

Exercise:

*Using objects that can stack (rocks, books, boxes, containers, pillows, etc), stack them slowly and carefully until they fall.*

*When the stack collapses, smile and laugh.*

The lives of many people are spent stacking things for the goal of success, as defined by society. People stack possessions, knowledge, relationships, degrees, money, jobs, toys, businesses, experiences, etc. They stress, fight, fatigue, compete, become ill, and get anxious and depressed through the process of stacking; yet, few people have found happiness. Society tells us that if our stack is high and mighty, we'll have obtained success - what a deception. What do you regret not stacking? How does your regret feed off the deception of stacking?

Allow the stack to fall. This lesson is not encouraging complacency; but instead teaches that real, authentic, and fulfilling experiences can only happen apart from the stress and worry of stacking. When you stack, you're focused on the future and the perceived importance of the stack; and then you have to maintain that heap of nonsense, which requires a lot of anxiety and pressure. Focus on your experience in the present moment; and if the stack falls, then smile and laugh.

*15 minutes of silence and focused breathing. Repeat the mantra: *"I allow the stack to fall."*

# Day 28

(Share this experience using #30DaysCandle)

Exercise:

*Light a candle and observe its flame for 5 minutes. Watch it move and feel its heat. Appreciate its energy.*

*Now, blow out the flame.*

*(If you don't have a candle, light a match and blow it out; and if you don't have a candle or match, stare at a dim light for 5 minutes and then turn it off.)*

The temperature of a small candle flame (and match flame) is around 1200 Celsius (which is about 2000 Fahrenheit). That's a lot of energy! And within a fraction of a second, it was extinguished as you blew it out; or in the case of the light, turned off its energy source. There wasn't a gradual process with delays and stops. You blew out the highly energized flame, and that was it - from 1200 Celsius to nonexistent in no time; or should I say, in present no time.

We think that our thoughts and feelings have so much energy and power. It's not just the illusion of regret, but all adverse attachments survive on this deception of power. The truth is: thoughts and attachments don't have energy like the candle flame, though your mind may have been tricked into believing they do. The candle flame is real and powerful; whereas most thoughts are illusory and fictitious.

As easily and quickly as you extinguished the flame, you can drop regret in the present moment.

*15 minutes of silence and focused breathing. Repeat the mantra: **"Dependency isn't real. It can be extinguished."**

# Day 29
(Share this experience using #30DaysLaugh)

Exercise:

*Make yourself laugh for 5 minutes. Don't stop laughing. You might feel strange, weird, embarrassed, or stupid...it doesn't matter, just laugh. Try to laugh alone and without the aid of a comedy or joke. If you don't know how to start, just start making the noises that typically accompany your laughter.*

What feelings did you experience during this exercise? Many people report feeling embarrassed or goofy, which is great; however, most people also report a feeling of relief and buoyancy when they've completed this exercise.

Similar to holding a smile, laughing for 5 minutes is a fantastic way to come into present awareness. If you think about it, humor is necessary for life. How sad is the person who is unable to laugh at the experiences of life? After all, life is funny, even the dreadful and lousy experiences.

If you ever again experience adverse thoughts and feelings that accompany regret, simply laugh at them. Consider how crazy and frivolous it is to have regret, and your reactions to it; it really is a funny misperception. No other living thing on the planet gets bothered by a misconception of past experiences. The entire situation is comical. If you perceive regret for what it truly is - a fictitious, impractical, and frivolous idea – then it can be easily dropped. You must learn to laugh at it. Genuinely laugh the regret away.

*15 minutes of silence and focused breathing. Repeat the mantra: **"Life is wonderful, funny, and real."**

# Day 30

(Share this experience using #30DaysThanks)

Exercise:

*Take a piece of paper (one that you can keep) and write down all that you are grateful for – these things don't have to be in any particular order of importance.*

*Next to each thing you list, write "Thank you."*

The person who isn't thankful for all that life gives is typically quite miserable; and regret thrives on that negativity. The truly grateful person can let go of anything at anytime. A thankful person is always a happy person, so practice gratitude daily.

Have you ever heard anyone say, *"I'm so grateful for feeling regret"*? Nobody is thankful for regret; which is a clear sign that it's an unhealthy misperception. However, a few people have learned to be thankful for the present moment experience.

Not only is it unhealthy, but an attachment to regret discourages a grateful mind and soul. With only one life to live in the present moment, it's important to always emphasize a grateful heart. Spend time with people who are grateful, and do things that nourish a thankful heart in the present moment. Anything that encourages misery and depression isn't worth giving attention to. Be thankful, always.

*15 minutes of silence and focused breathing. Repeat the mantra: **"I am grateful. I am thankful."**

# Conclusion

The exercises and lessons in this program taught and encouraged observation, awareness to your present moment experience, change of perception, and awakening to true happiness, which can only be found here and now. You were shown that your negative thoughts and feelings are not caused by regret, or any unhealthy misperception or attachment, but are solely within you and illusory; which means that you are capable of letting those thoughts and feelings pass and dropping regret in the present moment.

As mentioned at the beginning, there were no goals or measures of success for this program. If you were hoping to find validation or courage to fight an attachment, then you may be spending too much time struggling and thinking about regret. This was not meant to be a struggle or competition, but a release. You don't need to gain freedom; you already have it.

Life is not meant to be spent dealing with regret, or any type of unhealthy misperception. Wake up to the present moment and enjoy your present experience. If you've made it through the program, you are certainly more awakened then when you started; however, don't give up mindfully practicing observation of thoughts and feelings, stillness, silence, deep and focused breathing, allowing everything to pass, laughing, smiling, and being grateful.

Live wonderfully awakened and aware…with or without regret.

## *Notes for Day 1*
(Use this page to write down thoughts, reminders, ideas, prayers, mantras, revelations, lessons, modifications to the exercise, or experiences. If you'd like to share something, please post using **#30DaysNow** or use the exercise's unique hashtag.)

(40)

# *Notes for Day 2*

(Use this page to write down thoughts, reminders, ideas, prayers, mantras, revelations, lessons, modifications to the exercise, or experiences. If you'd like to share something, please post using **#30DaysNow** or use the exercise's unique hashtag.)

# *Notes for Day 3*

(Use this page to write down thoughts, reminders, ideas, prayers, mantras, revelations, lessons, modifications to the exercise, or experiences. If you'd like to share something, please post using **#30DaysNow** or use the exercise's unique hashtag.)

(44)

# *Notes for Day 4*

(Use this page to write down thoughts, reminders, ideas, prayers, mantras, revelations, lessons, modifications to the exercise, or experiences. If you'd like to share something, please post using **#30DaysNow** or use the exercise's unique hashtag.)

# *Notes for Day 5*

(Use this page to write down thoughts, reminders, ideas, prayers, mantras, revelations, lessons, modifications to the exercise, or experiences. If you'd like to share something, please post using **#30DaysNow** or use the exercise's unique hashtag.)

# *Notes for Day 6*

(Use this page to write down thoughts, reminders, ideas, prayers, mantras, revelations, lessons, modifications to the exercise, or experiences. If you'd like to share something, please post using **#30DaysNow** or use the exercise's unique hashtag.)

(50)

## *Notes for Day 7*
(Use this page to write down thoughts, reminders, ideas, prayers, mantras, revelations, lessons, modifications to the exercise, or experiences. If you'd like to share something, please post using **#30DaysNow** or use the exercise's unique hashtag.)

## *Notes for Day 8*
(Use this page to write down thoughts, reminders, ideas, prayers, mantras, revelations, lessons, modifications to the exercise, or experiences. If you'd like to share something, please post using **#30DaysNow** or use the exercise's unique hashtag.)

# *Notes for Day 9*

(Use this page to write down thoughts, reminders, ideas, prayers, mantras, revelations, lessons, modifications to the exercise, or experiences. If you'd like to share something, please post using **#30DaysNow** or use the exercise's unique hashtag.)

## Notes for Day 10

(Use this page to write down thoughts, reminders, ideas, prayers, mantras, revelations, lessons, modifications to the exercise, or experiences. If you'd like to share something, please post using **#30DaysNow** or use the exercise's unique hashtag.)

(58)

## *Notes for Day 11*

(Use this page to write down thoughts, reminders, ideas, prayers, mantras, revelations, lessons, modifications to the exercise, or experiences. If you'd like to share something, please post using **#30DaysNow** or use the exercise's unique hashtag.)

# Notes for Day 12

(Use this page to write down thoughts, reminders, ideas, prayers, mantras, revelations, lessons, modifications to the exercise, or experiences. If you'd like to share something, please post using **#30DaysNow** or use the exercise's unique hashtag.)

## *Notes for Day 13*

(Use this page to write down thoughts, reminders, ideas, prayers, mantras, revelations, lessons, modifications to the exercise, or experiences. If you'd like to share something, please post using **#30DaysNow** or use the exercise's unique hashtag.)

## *Notes for Day 14*

(Use this page to write down thoughts, reminders, ideas, prayers, mantras, revelations, lessons, modifications to the exercise, or experiences. If you'd like to share something, please post using **#30DaysNow** or use the exercise's unique hashtag.)

# *Notes for Day 15*

(Use this page to write down thoughts, reminders, ideas, prayers, mantras, revelations, lessons, modifications to the exercise, or experiences. If you'd like to share something, please post using **#30DaysNow** or use the exercise's unique hashtag.)

## *Notes for Day 16*

(Use this page to write down thoughts, reminders, ideas, prayers, mantras, revelations, lessons, modifications to the exercise, or experiences. If you'd like to share something, please post using **#30DaysNow** or use the exercise's unique hashtag.)

## *Notes for Day 17*

(Use this page to write down thoughts, reminders, ideas, prayers, mantras, revelations, lessons, modifications to the exercise, or experiences. If you'd like to share something, please post using **#30DaysNow** or use the exercise's unique hashtag.)

# Notes for Day 18

(Use this page to write down thoughts, reminders, ideas, prayers, mantras, revelations, lessons, modifications to the exercise, or experiences. If you'd like to share something, please post using **#30DaysNow** or use the exercise's unique hashtag.)

## *Notes for Day 19*

(Use this page to write down thoughts, reminders, ideas, prayers, mantras, revelations, lessons, modifications to the exercise, or experiences. If you'd like to share something, please post using **#30DaysNow** or use the exercise's unique hashtag.)

## *Notes for Day 20*

(Use this page to write down thoughts, reminders, ideas, prayers, mantras, revelations, lessons, modifications to the exercise, or experiences. If you'd like to share something, please post using **#30DaysNow** or use the exercise's unique hashtag.)

## *Notes for Day 21*

(Use this page to write down thoughts, reminders, ideas, prayers, mantras, revelations, lessons, modifications to the exercise, or experiences. If you'd like to share something, please post using **#30DaysNow** or use the exercise's unique hashtag.)

# *Notes for Day 22*

(Use this page to write down thoughts, reminders, ideas, prayers, mantras, revelations, lessons, modifications to the exercise, or experiences. If you'd like to share something, please post using **#30DaysNow** or use the exercise's unique hashtag.)

## *Notes for Day 23*
(Use this page to write down thoughts, reminders, ideas, prayers, mantras, revelations, lessons, modifications to the exercise, or experiences. If you'd like to share something, please post using **#30DaysNow** or use the exercise's unique hashtag.)

## *Notes for Day 24*

(Use this page to write down thoughts, reminders, ideas, prayers, mantras, revelations, lessons, modifications to the exercise, or experiences. If you'd like to share something, please post using **#30DaysNow** or use the exercise's unique hashtag.)

# Notes for Day 25

(Use this page to write down thoughts, reminders, ideas, prayers, mantras, revelations, lessons, modifications to the exercise, or experiences. If you'd like to share something, please post using **#30DaysNow** or use the exercise's unique hashtag.)

## *Notes for Day 26*

(Use this page to write down thoughts, reminders, ideas, prayers, mantras, revelations, lessons, modifications to the exercise, or experiences. If you'd like to share online, please post using **#30DaysNow** or use the exercise's unique hashtag.)

## *Notes for Day 27*

(Use this page to write down thoughts, reminders, ideas, prayers, mantras, revelations, lessons, modifications to the exercise, or experiences. If you'd like to share something, please post using **#30DaysNow** or use the exercise's unique hashtag.)

## *Notes for Day 28*

(Use this page to write down thoughts, reminders, ideas, prayers, mantras, revelations, lessons, modifications to the exercise, or experiences. If you'd like to share something, please post using **#30DaysNow** or use the exercise's unique hashtag.)

## Notes for Day 29

(Use this page to write down thoughts, reminders, ideas, prayers, mantras, revelations, lessons, modifications to the exercise, or experiences. If you'd like to share something, please post using **#30DaysNow** or use the exercise's unique hashtag.)

## *Notes for Day 30*

(Use this page to write down thoughts, reminders, ideas, prayers, mantras, revelations, lessons, modifications to the exercise, or experiences. If you'd like to share something, please post using **#30DaysNow** or use the exercise's unique hashtag.)

**To be mindful is to experience life in the present moment...it's the only moment we have.**

*Don't forget to leave an online review.*

*Thank you!*

Made in the USA
Columbia, SC
05 July 2023